BRIDE IDEAS AND FROCK-UPS

"There is no more lovely, friendly and charming relationship, communion or company than a good marriage."

Martin Luther (1483-1546)

BRIDE IDEAS AND FROCK-UPS

A book of wedding tips and slips

~

Sim Canetty-Clarke Amanda Lockhart
Susannah Frieze

Bene Factum Publishing
London

Bride Ideas and Frock-ups
A book of wedding tips and slips
First published in 2009 by
Bene Factum Publishing Ltd
PO Box 58122
London
SW8 5WZ

Email: inquiries@bene-factum.co.uk
www.bene-factum.co.uk

ISBN: 978-1-903071-22-9

Design and Typesetting by Eddie Ephraums, Envisage Books.
Printed in Slovenia on behalf of Latitude Press Limited.

"Sometimes, the one thing you are looking for
is the one thing you can't see."
Anon

CONTENTS

~

PRE-NUP

~

This book is so brilliant that it could almost persuade me to get married.

We live in a world where we are constantly told what we must do to achieve perfection. Sim, Amanda and Susannah don't tell anyone what to do. *Bride Ideas & Frock-Ups* is as far away from a 'How To', Martha Stewart-style lecture as I am from the demure bridal type. And that's why I love it… rifling through its rich tapestry of trivia, gasping at the antics of my fellow celebrities (even *moi* didn't know that Britney Spears had a cash bar at her own wedding) and shaking my head at all the absurd superstitions designed to trip up or set you on the path to eternal good luck.

Bride Ideas & Frock-Ups celebrates not just the bride and groom, but the whole cast list of hundreds for the Big Day. It's like a good blockbuster – sex, death, rock'n'roll – and your best ever history lesson, all rolled into one. And the pictures will just play havoc with your make-up. I have drooled over them: no frozen perfection here but a cheeky glimpse behind the scenes, from bridesmaids kicking up their heels, to ushers kicking up their skirts (yes, welcome to the 21st century, you read that right), it's an emotional rollercoaster of a day – and we are there for every gripping twist and turn.

I want to buy this book for all my friends and family – for the marrieds, as a trip down Memory Lane, for the unmarrieds, to show them that the whole prospect of matrimony need not be so dauntingly perfect, for my gay boys, included so effortlessly – for anyone who thinks a wedding is just about a big white dress.

As Mae West said, "Marriage is a great institution. But I'm not ready for an institution yet." I'm with Mae, but for now, you'll find me happily tucked up with *Bride Ideas & Frock-Ups*…

Tara ♡

Tara Palmer-Tomkinson

Introduction

A MOST HONOURABLE ESTATE

~

"The first bond of society is marriage."
Cicero (106-43 BC)

Births, weddings and deaths – the 'hatched, matched and despatched' of newspaper column fame – are the very stuff of life, but there's no need to be deadly serious about any of them. We'll leave it to someone else to put the mirth into birth and the belly laughs into bereavement, but we are here to debunk the awesome majesty of this most honourable estate and render the Big Day a bit less Big and Scary. "Marriage means being committed," goes the saying, "but then again so does insanity". We say, let's fling open the doors of the asylum and show marriage for what it is, warts and winsomeness and all.

"The most wonderful of all things in life is the discovery of another human being with whom one's relationship has a glowing depth, beauty, and joy as the years increase… it cannot be found by looking for it… it is a sort of Divine accident." – Sir Hugh Walpole (1884-1941)

In a 2007 survey, six out of ten polled believed in love at first sight, with as many as a million saying they would propose immediately if they found 'the one'…

But steady there, tiger, for then start the formalities. Like the banns, read out in church on the three Sundays before the wedding (from the Old English word, 'to summon'), designed to allow anyone to raise a legal objection to the marriage. Not only could bigamy be avoided, but this way couples didn't topple headlong – or clandestinely – into marriage: this way the banns "deterred dowry hunters, carpetbaggers and general Jack the Lads who preyed upon eligible, well off and naïve women."

I told a friend I was getting married and he said, 'Have you picked a date yet?' I said, 'Wow, you can bring a date to your own wedding? What a country!' – Yakov Smirnoff, comedian.

"By all means marry. If you get a good wife, you will be very happy; if you get a bad one, you will become a philosopher — and that is good for any man."

Socrates (469-399 BC)

It was early days in the process of the world's Creation that God realised the fatal flaw if Adam were left enjoying the bachelor lifestyle, as well as tacitly admitting that the poor First Man simply couldn't cope on his own… "The Lord God said, 'It is not good for man to be alone. I will make a helper suitable for him.'"– Genesis 2:18

"We adore chaos because we love to produce order." – M.C. Escher (1898-1972)

In Roman times, marriage was deliberately designed for the production of legitimate children and was considered to be at the very heart of society's future. In a move that would strike fear into the hearts of today's commitment-phobes, Emperor Augustus (63 BC-AD 14) even set penalties for men who were single for long periods of time. Perhaps this should still be enforced…

"Her pulse beats matrimony." – John Ray, *English Proverbs*, 1732

'Tying the knot' may suggest a negative view of wedlock, being shackled to the ball and chain, bundled into bondage and other such tempting metaphors, but has more charming roots… Back in Roman times, the bride would wear a girdle that was tied in many knots which the groom had the 'duty' of untying. Knowing the average man's ability to pop a bra clasp, the mind boggles…

What we mean by tying the knot, however, is based on the Celtic tradition of 'hand-fasting' – tying a knot around a couple's clasped hands, knots being the image of hope, fidelity and even good luck… Which was fortunate for one of our more rain-soaked brides. The bridal party was waiting disconsolately in the lychgate of the church, waiting to sprint up the path to the church, when up hove a villager. "Don't fret, pet," he said, looking at our bride's woebegone face, "there's nowt wrong with rain - a wet knot is harder to untie."

"Marriage is when a man and woman become as one; the trouble starts when they try to decide which one." – Anon

Betrothal was the big thing both throughout the Bible, the Jewish Talmud and, in England, from the time of the Anglo-Saxons right into the deepest Middle Ages: as long as a kiss was exchanged at public espousal, the match was legally binding – the only release being if one of the couple died. Serial engagers take note.

"Dear George, I have waited three years for you, but now I have met a GI. We are going to get married but don't worry too much because he says when you come home, he will buy you the motorbike you always wanted. Love, Jill." – Letter to a British soldier in a POW camp, 1944

"Everything about marriage, and above all romantic marriage, will continue to fascinate until kissing goes out of fashion."
Arthur May, Marriage a la Mode, 1925

Marriage mania in the 20th century took a sinister turn with the advent of the mass wedding, the largest of which was conducted by the Rev Sun Myung Moon in Seoul, Korea, in 1988: 6,516 Moonie couples in the romantic surroundings of a huge factory building, all reciting their wedding vows at the same time. Nothing like making it a special day…

"All tragedies are finished by a death / All comedies are ended by a marriage." – Lord Byron (1788-1824)

In the 21st century, the celebrity wedding has come of age. Celebrity magazines are bankrolling the phenomenon; the lunacy reached its peak with the unseemly jostling over the nuptials of footballer Wayne Rooney and Coleen McLoughlin. Ever-eager *Hello!* bid around £1.5m but were trumped by the proprietor of *OK!* mag with "the biggest cheque I've ever written"- a whopping £2.5m. Lucky *OK!* readers were then treated to over 100 pages, spread over three issues…

Celebrity Wedding Overload is now a recognised bar to the happiness of ordinary couples planning their wedding. "Everyone sees the designer goodies the A-listers have," warns a prominent wedding planner, "and they think they need all these expensive things to somehow make their wedding 'special.'" In a recent survey, one in ten UK couples admitted to taking on an extra part-time job beforehand in an effort to bring 'celeb' touches to their wedding… We say, save yourselves the effort: bringing unceleb touches like fidelity and enduring love is better than a bling-encrusted chocolate fountain any day.

"Good marriages are seldom celebrated, while every tiff or spat in a celebrity marriage becomes tabloid fodder." – Hillary Rodham Clinton, 1996

In a recent survey by Alliance & Leicester, total wedding spending was up at £23 billion just for that year. The average wedding costs over £17,000, from engagement ring to honeymoon, even though, between 1971 and 1999, the number of marriages decreased by 35%. In contrast to a few decades ago, 93% do not think that their parents would foot the bill: most brides expected to be in debt by £10,000 after their wedding day.

In a bid to have the cheapest wedding of their peers, one couple spent only £500 on the whole day, after an appeal in the local paper. Tables, chairs, decorations, wedding cake, a huge curry, even cash for their honeymoon were all donated by family, friends and local tradesmen for the 40-guest registry service and barn-held reception. "We didn't want to go to our parents and demand thousands of pounds for a wedding; we'd rather do it this way, scraping together for a totally unique day."

Celebrity Wedding Costs

• Liza Minelli's wedding to David Gest cost $3.4million – and the wedding lasted 16 months. Which is the equivalent of Liza saying, "I won't get out of bed and be married for anything less than $7,000 a day,": quite good value compared to certain supermodels…

• Catherine Zeta Jones and Michael Douglas's wedding cost £1.5million – £500 per head catering costs (they knew what they were up against with those Welsh drinkers…) and a dress that cost £100,000. The cake alone cost £7,000 – then inadvertently a lot more: it was the unauthorised photos of a diet-starved CZJ gorging on it that caused the infamous court case afterwards. Still, the Douglases ended up making £1million in legal awards – which helped out.

• The total cost of Prince Charles's wedding to Princess Diana was finally estimated to be in the £35million ball park – and was watched by more than 750 million viewers – thereby making it one of the century's cheaper blockbusters.

• At Madonna and Guy Ritchie's ill-fated £1.5million wedding, the champagne alone cost £200,000 lock, stock and crate.

• Canny Joan Collins actually made a profit on her wedding to toyboy Percy Gibson. While the marriage cost a mere £100,000, the deal with *OK!* magazine netted the happy couple £375,000. No wonder our favourite diva was spotted doing a giddy conga with her guests at Claridge's…

• History doesn't relate how much Britney Spears's wedding to Kevin Federline set her back… but costs were clearly defrayed by the fact that at her reception, one of the world's richest popstars restricted her guests to a cash bar…

Since 1992, there have been more civil ceremonies in England and Wales than religious – 66% versus 34%.

Peggy Guggenheim was asked how many husbands she had had. "My own or other people's?" she replied.

Paying for the wedding is now a pragmatic matter of deciding who is best placed to afford it – but it used to be the domain of the father of the bride. In the 18th century, the notices of marriages in newspapers actually used to give the pound value of the bride's fortune, dating back to when a father provided his daughter with a dowry to tempt a man into marrying her… in *King Lear*, one of Cordelia's suitors falls away when he hears that she will have no dowry.

"I didn't want five husbands, but it happened that way and that's all there is to it."
Rita Hayworth (1918-1987)

Famous People Who Have Liked Getting Married

9 – Zsa Zsa Gabor
8 – Elizabeth Taylor
8 – Mickey Rooney
6 – Gloria Swanson
6 – Henry VIII
5 – Richard Burton
5 – Clark Gable
5 – Judy Garland
4 – Humphrey Bogart
4 – Charlie Chaplin
4 – Patsy Kensit
3 – Marilyn Monroe
3 – Jennifer Lopez
3 – Rod Stewart

"On quiet nights, when I'm alone, I like to run our wedding video backwards, just to watch myself walk out of the church a free man." – Jim Davidson (married three times)

An Edwardian Woman's Chance To Marry

14.5% from 15-20 years of age
52% from 20-25 years of age
18% from 25-30 years of age
15.5% from 30-35 years of age
3.75% from 35-40 years of age
2.5% from 40-45 years of age
0.375% from 45-50 years of age
0.25% from 50-56 years of age
– from *Romance of the Zanigs*
(a wedding how-to book, popular in 1904)

"Shotgun wedding – a matter of wife or death." – Anon

Reasons not to let your wedding be taken over by paparazzi (just in case you were verging on being jealous of celebrities' luxey weddings):

• **The bin bags:** the mag readers must be the first to see the wedding dress… so stars have been known to arrive in gorgeous cars – but with windows blacked out by bin bags – or, like Claudia Schiffer, they allow the vast sums they receive from *Hello!* to go to their head – literally – as when she left her hotel shrouded in hotel blankets and hemmed in by burly security guards. One of the crowd of waiting fans said, "When we realised we weren't going to see anything of her, everyone just started booing."

• **The camera issue:** unauthorised photos are the bane of any exclusive magazine deal - but hunting for hidden cameras doesn't make anyone feel welcome… at the Beckham bash, Posh's mum was frisked. Even the £1m from *OK!* doesn't get round the fact that this is not the way to soften up your future mother-in-law…

• **General overdose of security:** as at the Rooney wedding, with a rumoured two security guards per guest, or at Paul Gascoigne's wedding, covered by *Hello!*, when actual fights broke out between guests and overzealous security guards. At CZJ's wedding to Michael Douglas, she was held up for ten minutes by her own security detail as they were still doing their 'perimeter sweep'…

• **Even security tagging your guests:** at Posh Spice and David Beckham's wedding, all 236 guests wore a tag to flush out gatecrashers, even the couple's baby son Brooklyn.

• **Getting your priorities right:** at the Beckhams' wedding, the bride and groom stayed up until dawn, editing photos with the *OK!* team. Mmm, sounds like fun.

• **That step too far:** when Grant Bovey and Anthea Turner appeared on the cover of *OK!* at their wedding reception, eating and appearing to endorse Snowflakes chocolate bars, it was the death knell of their own B-List celebrity.

• **The honeymoon:** some glossy mag deals are a 'two-fer' – wedding and honeymoon for the price of one. So wave goodbye to privacy, kicking back and allowing that spot you kept at bay for the ceremony to finally have its moment: it's full make-up and shiny smiles for the camera, please…

"The concept of two people living together for 25 years… suggests a lack of spirit only to be admired in sheep." – columnist Alan Patrick Herbert

"*Men marry to make an end; women to make a beginning.*"
Alexis Dupuy

– I –

THE BEST LAID PLANS
Controlling the uncontrollable

❦

"Most marriages are not made in heaven.
They come in kit form and you put them together yourselves."
Alfred Tennyson (1809-1892)

With eight out of ten brides-to-be wanting a formal wedding, the frenzy of planning and orgy of detail in the months that mark the trough between the peaks of pleasure that are betrothal and the wedding: all these will be familiar to any bride and groom. During this period (the average engagement lasts nine months), it seems impossible to think about anything else than the crucial, superstition-riddled decisions to make about the Big Day, to the point where the bride's original personality can seem to alter... something we now call the Bridezilla Phenomenon.

The planning fuss was ever thus, as in this passage from *Home Thoughts* in 1901. "She was simply a dear, sweet girl until she named her wedding-day. From the tying of her shoe-string to the glitter of her costliest wedding gift… by the eve of the wedding, there was literally no other thing thought of but the event and its central, white-robed figure."

"How can a woman be expected to be happy with a man who insists on treating her as if she were a perfectly normal human being?" – Oscar Wilde (1854-1900)

Even the path to engagement is fraught with mumbo-jumbo…in times past, if, on the way to propose to his lady love, the would-be groom encountered a blind person, a pregnant woman or a monk, the marriage was then believed to be doomed, the latter because of their association with poverty and chastity. Buying the engagement and wedding rings at the same time is also thought to bring bad luck.

"Marriage is not simply a meal ticket; it binds your mind, your body, your thoughts." – Sylvia and Peter Duncan, *How To Be A Better Wife*, 1956

"Thus grief still treads upon the heels of pleasure —
Marry'd in haste, we may repent at leisure.
Some by experience find those words misplaced;
At leisure marry, they repent in haste."

William Congreve (1670-1729)

"Always get married early in the morning. That way, if it doesn't work out, you haven't wasted a whole day."
Mickey Rooney (married eight times…)

"Matrimony. The high sea for which no compass has yet been invented."
The Bride's Book, 1901

Things You Never Even Knew You Had To Plan For…

- **Hair colour:** "A man with very light flax-coloured hair or a man with deep red hair should not marry a woman with hair of the same colour… for it will be fearfully bad for the children." – *Young Men and Women of America*, 1871

- **Name:** Change the name, not the letter – You'll change for worse and not for better – proverb

- **Age:** "I believe the marriage stands the best chance when the bride is between 20-25 and the bridegroom a year or two older. Grafted together in youth, two loves grow and merge together…" Sylvia and Peter Duncan, *How To Be A Better Wife*, 1956

- **Moon:** "An eclipse on a wedding day means that one half of the couple will block out the other. It also means the blocking out of royalty. For Charles and Camilla, the eclipse on their wedding day means that Charles will never be king." – Italian astrologer Branko. Marrying under a waxing moon will mean your happiness will increase and increase but it's even better under a full moon: you and your spouse will have full lives, full pockets and full hearts….

- **Strange Mandatory Payments:** In Germany there is the bizarre compulsory fee of £22 known as 'bigamy insurance' – so that the registrar's office can check that you are both free to marry.

Traditionally, six weeks before a Nigerian woman married, she must over-eat in an attempt to fatten herself up: the more girth she could heave towards her ogling groom on the Big Day, the better. She was segregated away from the rest of the family and fed high-calorie porridge by the older women… Meanwhile, the wedding present of choice from groom to bride was, appositely enough, a metal cooking pot as big as he could possibly afford…

"Planning a wedding is like doing cartwheels or using chopsticks – it looks easy til you try it." – Anon

One would-be bride planned her wedding so minutely that she got herself into the newspapers – for missing out one crucial detail: the bridegroom. She had a Chantilly lace dress designed, picked the venue, chose the music for the first dance, created her perfect bouquet, chose the lingerie she'd wear on her wedding night and saved £5,000 in a 'wedding day' account – all before she'd even found a boyfriend. "I'm passionate about weddings," she told reporters. "I daydream about my own. Of course I need a groom before I get married, but I'll meet Mr Right one day. In the meantime, why not start preparing?"

Planning Ahead and Getting Priorities Right: a personal column in the *Morning Advertiser*, "Ex-London publican seeks lady with pub for marriage. Send photo of pub."

Wed on Monday, always poor,
Wed on Tuesday, wed once more,
Wed on Wednesday, happy match,
Wed on Thursday, splendid catch,
Wed on Friday, poorly mated,
Wed on Saturday, better waited.

The wedding planner is a phenomenon of the modern age, laid down for posterity in films like *Father of the Bride* (the outrageously true-to-shocking-reality Franck) and the limply eponymous *Wedding Planner*. But even in New York in 1865, there was nothing a good planner couldn't procure, as advised by Robert de Valcourt in his *Illustrated Manners*: "All you have to say is, 'Mr Brown, a little wedding party at my house on the 17th – say, about 200 people, and cost – well, 600 dollars.' It will be done, and if your visiting list is short of the requisite number, Mr Brown will furnish you guests of the most unexceptionable style and deportment – dancing gentlemen, supper men, literary, artistic."

"I had to face some very difficult spending decisions and I've had to conduct sensitive diplomacy. That's called planning for a wedding." – George W. Bush begins to find his natural level of operations…

Celine Dion's wedding to her producer Rene Angelil, 26 years her senior, was planned like a major musical production: they employed over 800 people to work full-time for three months… and that still didn't avert a last minute crisis about the dress – 90 yards of heavily appliquéd and beaded silk and lace which took over 1,000 hours to make and which was finally finished at 2am on the morning of the wedding.

Watch out for the wildlife: superstitious tosh or natural checklist for things to look out for on the way to the church?

Good Luck: a lamb, a goat , a dove, a wolf (!), a spider or a toad.

Bad Luck: a pig, a priest, a monk, a dog, a cat, a hare, a lizard or serpent – even a passing funeral procession or an open grave.

If a flock of birds flies over the bride's car, she will have lots of children, though the traditional instruction to count them to see how many may make her feel a little faint at the prospect…

A Japanese groom comes to the ceremony accompanied by two waddling ducks, or a goose and gander: because they mate for life, they represent fidelity.

"Keep your eyes wide open before the wedding, half shut afterwards."
Benjamin Franklin (1706-1790)

"The best laid plans o' mice…

. . .an' men. . ." – Robbie Burns (1759-1796)

– II –

DOES MY BUM LOOK BIG IN THIS?
The bride getting ready

∾

"The critical period of the day of matrimony is breakfast time."
The Institution of Marriage, Sir Alan Patrick Herbert (1890-1971)

The language of clothes and accessories on a wedding day is a complicated minefield of superstition, one-upmanship, tradition and fashion, at the end of which a happy bride will look radiant anyway, were she plain as a pikestaff or cover-girl gorgeous. Even the addition of a veil, or flowers, or the very colour of the dress has their own meaning or superstition. The good news is that a bride can usually just sit back and enjoy the ride: this is the one day of her life when she can expect to be a little pampered by those around her....

Wearing a white dress is rooted in Roman times, when a bride wore a simple white shift set off by a girdle, veil and sandals that were dyed a deep saffron yellow – yellow being the colour of Hymen, goddess of fertility and prosperity, who presided over weddings.

It wasn't until Queen Victoria married Prince Albert in 1840 that the white wedding dress became a tradition – before that there was no customary bridal colour: a bride merely wore her best dress. Victoria will not have chosen white for its associations with virginity and Biblical modesty; the colour more usually associated with that was the blue of a thousand Madonna depictions – though thereafter white was associated with her innocence. No, more prosaically, she most likely selected it because, from the early 19th century, it was the fashion for white to be worn for formal occasions. In doing so, she actually went against the fashion for royal brides (as a show of their wealth and majesty) to wear silver or cloth of gold on their wedding day.

Paula Yates married in bright red satin; Marilyn Monroe contradicted her sultry screen image in a demure dark brown suit; Jordan wed in lurid pink.

"A dress that zips up at the back will bring a husband and wife together."
American statesman James H. Boren

One weird belief that persisted into the early 19th century was that, if a woman was married in the simplest undyed linen smock, then her husband could not be held responsible for any debts contracted by her before the marriage; he would be taking her without apparent 'worldly goods', with her debts thus left behind.

Katie Price (aka Jordan) had no thoughts of wearing a smock when she married popstrel Peter André and, as the major breadwinner, had no fear of debts, except perhaps in the taste department. Glittering head to foot in Swarovski crystals, from the top of her enormous pink crown to the bottom of her unashamed pink meringue (a relative snip at £20,000), she broke all records for her sheer blinging bravura… "It's so big, I can't bend my finger," she said of her 35-diamond wedding ring.

Sometimes it's just a case of remembering to bring everything – the jewellery, the tiara, the garter, all those crucial little accessories. One of our brides left it to the last minute to put on her dress. Meanwhile, her attendants had packed her bags ready for her honeymoon and left them for a taxi driver to take to the first night hotel. It was only after all the attendants had left for the church, mobiles turned off, that the bride came to put on her dress. No dress anywhere to be seen. The taxi driver had lumped everything together and taken the gown as well, leaving her dressed only in bra and pants, with no clue about what had happened…

"Does my bum look big in this?" "Your bum would need control pants with the holding power of Fort Knox not to look big in a wedding dress. Luckily for us all, no-one will be looking at your backside, they'll be looking at your face." A conversation overheard between mother and daughter, trying on dresses in a wedding shop.

Madonna nixed hats at her wedding as being 'too old-fashioned' but other celebs have let their fame go to their head: Mel B of the Spice Girls wore a diamanté and ostrich feather head dress, while her groom Jimmy Gulzar wore a jewelled Stetson. Posh Spice famously wore a crown that cost £10,000. Celine Dion's bizarre, ungainly wooden headpiece was covered with 2,000 Austrian crystals, weighed seven pounds and by the end of the day had cut into her scalp.

"*Love is blind. Marriage is the eye-opener.*"
Author Pauline Thomason

"I dreamed of a wedding of elaborate elegance; a church filled with flowers and friends.
I asked him what kind of wedding he wished for; he said one that would make me his wife."
Anon

An ambitious pastry-chef from the Ukraine wanted to show off his wares on his wedding day – so he made his fiancée's wedding dress: out of 1,500 cream puffs and caramel. It took the 28 year old groom three months to make – and at the end of the day his bride swore that she never wanted to take it off…. Good tucker for the honeymoon, presumably.

The bride should never wear all her wedding outfit – especially not the dress and the veil together – before the Big Day and even then should leave one or two stitches of the dress undone so that a 'good luck' stitch can be added to complete it as she leaves for the ceremony.

Don't scream. Finding a spider crawling on her wedding dress is a sign of very good luck for the bride. If she forgets this and sits down in shock anyway – and happens to do so on a piece of lamb's wool (as you do) – then she will have children with wavy hair…

The bridal veil – although part of Roman weddings and mentioned in the Bible – was re-introduced into Europe by returning Crusaders as a way to ward off 'the evil eye'. Wearing the veil worn by your grandmother means you will always have wealth. Accidentally tearing your veil is good luck, particularly if done so at the altar – though tell that to our bride whose bridesmaids trod so heavily on her veil as they followed her towards the altar, that she had whiplash and a pounding headache for the rest of her happy day. Sometimes a bride came to church with her hair loose and down around her face – "married in her hair" – it served the same purpose of protecting her from evil spirits and underlined her status as a virgin maiden.

Victorian adage: Something old, something new,
                      Something borrowed, something blue,
                      And a sixpence in the shoe.

• **Something old** to be from a happily married woman as a lucky transfer of happiness to the new bride: often the veil.

• **Something new** to be some aspect of the bride's new finery – and symbolised the new life she was about to embark upon.

• **Something borrowed** to be some object of gold to guarantee wealth in the future.

• **Something blue** is symbolic of the heavens, the colour of Biblical and Jewish purity and of the Virgin Mary.

• **Sixpence in the shoe** (besides slowing the bride down should she want to run away), to be worn in the heel of the left shoe to ensure prosperity, while the shoe here represents fertility.

"*Mamma brought me a Nosegay of orange flowers... I wore a white satin dress with a very deep flounce of Honiton lace, imitation of old. I wore my Turkish diamond necklace and earrings and Albert's beautiful sapphire brooch.*"

Queen Victoria, in her journal, 10th February, 1840

The coin that Wallis Simpson tucked into her left blue suede shoe on her wedding to the Duke of Windsor in 1937 was a gold coronation coin emblazoned with the face of her husband. Ironic that, given that it was because of her that six months' earlier Edward VIII had given up the throne only one year after the coronation so that he could marry her.

Married in blue, love ever true,
Married in white, you've chosen right,
Married in red, you'll wish yourself dead,
Married in black, you'll wish yourself back,
Married in gray, you'll go far away,
Married in brown, you'll live out of town,
Married in green, ashamed to be seen,
Married in pink, of you he'll aye think,
Married in pearl, you'll live in a whirl,
Married in yellow, jealous of your fellow.
– Mid 19th century rhyme

Just in case you wanted to be thrifty, don't. Nicole Kidman publicly rued her decision to use an old dress that she'd bought in an Amsterdam flea market for her wedding to Tom Cruise, and it is actively bad luck to make your own wedding gown.

Garters… Former *Baywatch* babe Traci Bingham brought a classy touch to her own wedding with a musical garter that played 'Here comes the Bride' from under her dress as she walked up the aisle…

Q. Why does the bride wear white?
A. To blend in with everything else in the kitchen.

Just Call Me Packhorse: Superstitious Items To Be Carried By The Bride

- Salt in her glove or shoe or pocket: abhorred by witches and devils, as a preservative it symbolises lasting friendship and loyalty
- Mother's prayer book
- Small stalks of wheat or corn stalks and leaves, to symbolise fruitfulness
- But it's bad luck (not to mention bad hygiene) to carry a handkerchief used by another bride

The bride's bouquet is another hotbed of superstition and symbolism. In the Middle Ages it was traditionally a protective talisman: a tightly bunched combination of garlic, chives, rosemary, bay and other strong and potent herbs, all carefully selected for their special powers against witches and demons – and the health hazards of gathering a mob of people together in an enclosed space. In ancient Poland, it was believed that sprinkling sugar on the bride's bouquet kept her temper sweet.

Elizabethans included rosemary for remembrance. For the Victorians, every flower chosen was a coded signal… lilacs and roses for love, lilies for purity, chrysanthemums as a symbol of truth. Red columbine was held to say, "I'm anxious and trembling," which can't really be a good thing to communicate on your wedding day.

Myrtle, associated with Venus, the goddess of love, has a long history of being included in the bridal bouquet. Many myrtle bushes, found in old cottage gardens, owe their existence to the country custom of planting a sprig of myrtle from the bride's bouquet as the wedding party returned from church. The planting was done by a bridesmaid: blooming presaged another wedding but if it did not grow, the planter would sadly be an old maid.

Tiaras are increasingly popular bridal accoutrements, though few are as magnificent as the sun ray fringe necklace inherited from George IV and made up as a tiara for our Queen Elizabeth's wedding day in 1947. When it fell apart on the wedding morning and the Crown jeweller had to be sent for, the then Princess Elizabeth was famously relaxed. As Princess Margaret once said, "My sister is the only person I know who can put on a tiara with one hand while going downstairs."

The world's most expensive dress has not yet been worn by a bride – but who could or would afford the pricetag of £8million for a dress that was designed by a jeweller and is stiff with diamonds?

"It is unlucky for the bride to look at herself in the glass after she is completely dressed; so the bride of today 'for fun' puts on a glove or other trifle of attire after the last look has been taken in the mirror."

Mrs Burton Kingsland, Etiquette for All Occasions, 1901

Princess Diana had an identical copy of her wedding dress made so that it could go on display at Madame Tussauds the day after the wedding. It was then sold on by the waxworks in 2005 for £100,000 after word got out that the Princess herself had worn it during fittings… Rather more than the £6,400 fetched for the Duchess of York's replica wedding dress or the £19 Asda charged for the imitation of the Duchess of Cornwall's engagement ring.

One post-war bride owed her mother for 'making do' on her wedding dress. She snapped up two unused WW2 silk parachutes for £2 each and used one for her eldest daughter's wedding dress and the other, dyed pink, for the bridesmaid's dress. "I wore mine again, for our 50th anniversary," the bride recalls, "it was merely a little yellowed."

Women do not corner the market when it comes to preening and primping for their wedding day. Vince Neil, of Mötley Crüe, had $70,000 worth of plastic surgery before his wedding while, in 2007, Pete Burns – former frontman of Dead or Alive and also no stranger to the surgeon's knife – was resplendent at his civil partnership ceremony, draped in a white kimono embellished with gold and crimson designs. Manicured hands sporting black nail varnish holding a scarlet fan completed the look.

Some brides' paranoia is well-placed. The mother of one of our brides came in to see her daughter just before she left for the church, took one look at her dress, and said, "Is that what you're wearing? Oh no! Really? I wouldn't have put you in that. It's not you at all." Thanks, Mum.

Sometimes the tension can get to a bride. One of our brides took a Mogadon because she wanted to make sure she got enough sleep the night before the wedding. She took one more for luck, overdid it and had to be physically propped up during the service and prompted at each turn by a vicar who was clearly in need of a Valium himself by the end of the ceremony.

"Let me not to the marriage of true minds
Admit impediments. Love is not love
Which alters when it alteration finds."
– William Shakespeare, Sonnet 116

GIRLS ALOUD
The bridesmaids

༄

"A happy bridesmaid makes a happy bride"
Alfred Tennyson, The Bridesmaid (1872)

At Jamaican weddings, the maid (or matron) of honour is known as The Chief and she is the one deferred to all day as the gatekeeper of the whole wedding. So it is in this chapter, where we pay homage to the selfless helpmeet that is the bridesmaid, the (usually) young woman who is close friend or sister to the bride. For the bride, her wedding day is the happiest of her life; for her bridesmaids, it is a day of work… getting the bride ready, avoiding all the superstitious pitfalls of pins, shoes, evil demons, cake-cutting and sock-throwing, while never, ever taking attention away from The Main Attraction. Bridesmaids, we salute you.

The job of bridesmaid has an ancient pedigree: in the Bible, in Genesis, Jacob's two wives Leah and Rachel (greedy boy, that Jacob) come to the ceremony with a named handmaiden each, while in Psalms 45:14, there is mention made of bridesmaids for a royal bride, Technicolour Dreamcoat-style: "In many-coloured robes, she is led to the king, with her virgin companions following behind her."

The most frequent number of bridesmaids is four, including the maid (or matron, if she is married herself) of honour. Nearly 62% of church weddings have little girls (or flower girls, as they are called over the pond) while 36% have a pageboy (or ringbearer).

Back in Anglo-Saxon times, it was the bride's maid's duty to escort the bride to church – and it was believed that the girl to whom this task was entrusted would herself be married within a year…. But be careful there in your Jimmy Choos: another adage holds that a bridesmaid who stumbled on the way to the altar would die an old maid.

"*Marriage. . . is a damnably serious business.*"
John Philips Marquand (1893-1960)

The custom of dressing bridesmaids in matching dresses goes back to the days when attendants acted as decoys, both to protect the bride from kidnap (when marriage by capture was still legal and marriageable women were scarce) and to shield the bride from the demons that were supposed to lurk at weddings. Demons being evil spirits of small brains, it was reasoned that if the bridesmaids dressed identically they would bamboozle the malevolent spirits and distract their eye from the veiled mystery woman in white…

Celebrity has become an equally distracting matter for the modern bride. When American Idol contestant Brooke White couldn't walk down the aisle at her sister's wedding because she was still singing in the reality TV competition, her replacement was a lifesize cardboard cut-out…

One of the more unusual 'jobs' for the bridesmaid was this – "Take a pound of Limburger cheese, spread between two towels, making a poultice. Place under the pillow of newlyweds on their first night, and good fortune and many offspring will be theirs." – *The Folklore of Weddings*, 1970

Part of the work description of a bridesmaid is to keep the bride together and sane throughout the day. Tell that to one of our brides, whose photographer arrived to snap her getting ready, and walked in to find the bride and her three bridesmaids lying on the bed in their finery, all hog-whimperingly drunk. When the father of the bride arrived, he was in an even worse state than his daughter. From then on, it was all just downhill… In the back of the Bentley all the way to the church, the daughter and dad continued to take swigs from his hip flask then, clinging on to each other for support and dear life, ricocheted off the pews up the very long aisle….

For grown-up bridesmaids, the Little Black Dress is increasingly their wedding retinue dress of choice, but this would have shocked past generations. "It is not considered lucky or appropriate to wear black at a wedding," thundered Mrs E W Sherwood, in her book, *Correct Social Usage*, 1906. "Even those who are in mourning among the ladies of the bride's family and bridal attendants should not wear black, but instead, a deep cardinal red."

While Queen Victoria had a royally impressive 12 bridesmaids, Liza Minnelli had no fewer than 15, most of whom were old enough to be grandmothers, including her matron of honour, Elizabeth Taylor (78 and wheelchair-bound), Esther Williams (78) of heart-shaped swimming pool fame, Gina Lollobrigida (73) and relative spring chicken Petula Clark who, at 69, apparently made a game attempt to leap up and catch the bouquet. Between them, the bridesmaids had a grand total of SIXTY marriages. We say, think of them positively as knowledgeable about wedding etiquette, not just as a motley crew of old boilers…

Czech bridesmaids have to arrive early on the wedding day, preferably dressed in wellies and overalls. Before they get into their finery, it is their job to plant a tree in the bride's garden (or, in modern times, more often windowsill), then decorate it with coloured ribbons and painted eggshells. Slovak legend believed that the bride would then live as long as the tree.

When Edward VIII (then Duke of Windsor) abdicated and was preparing for his wedding day, his young niece Princess Elizabeth had already been bridesmaid to his two other brothers and he naturally assumed that she would be bridesmaid at his nuptials. But it was not considered appropriate for any of his royal relations to even attend the civil wedding of the Duke and his twice-divorced bride, Mrs Simpson.

"Always pick ugly bridesmaids. There is nothing more devastating for the bride, who has taken months to make herself look as good as she can, than to see all the male guests ogling the bridesmaids instead of her... you're better off with a little flower girl or a pageboy — ideally, a pageboy who picks his nose."

Duffer's Guide to Getting Married, 1986

In Chinese tradition, the bride chooses a bridesmaid to come to her home the evening before the wedding to perform the hair-combing ritual. The bridesmaid combs out the bride's hair four times: first, for her life's journey from beginning to end; second, for lifelong harmony; third, for many sons and grandsons (daughters were, presumably, the nits that got thrown out along the way); fourth, for wealth and a long marriage.

With part of the bridesmaid's role to help fit the bride into the dress, trust Madonna not to allow for the possibility of error on her own wedding day by choosing, as her maid of honour, not Gwyneth Paltrow, as expected, but the very designer of her wedding dress, Stella McCartney.

As if it wasn't bad enough having a younger sister that was more beautiful and beguiling than you were, in Tudor England the older, unmarried sister of the bride had to dance barefoot at the wedding feast (sometimes even in a pig's trough, just to complete the self-esteem exercise) or it was said that she would remain an old maid.

At a traditional Sikh wedding, being a bridesmaid means getting your hands dirty. Before the bride leaves her house, five bridesmaids must dip their hands in a mix of oil, turmeric and other spices and leave five handprints on the wall of her room as a lucky sign.

When two bridesmaids flew in the night before a wedding in Antigua, their luggage (containing their bridesmaids' dresses) was lost. The next day, this being the Caribbean, the taxi that the airline sent with the located bags was an hour late – by which time the bride was having the vapours and the wedding guests inside the church were getting restless and hot. "The other bridesmaid and I literally wrenched the door open before the taxi had even stopped, pulled our dresses from our suitcases, and stripped right there in front of the church to get into them," said one, "leaving the rather chastened taxi driver meekly stuffing all our other belongings back into the bags."

Urban myths we hate: the one where, at the fateful 'let them speak now' moment of the ceremony, the bride thanks the maid of honour for sleeping with the groom the night before…

The behaviour of small bridesmaids and pageboys at weddings is legendarily bad. At one of our American weddings, the flower girl (aged 4) and the pageboy (an ambitious 2) entirely forgot that they were meant to scatter the petals as they walked and just wrestled over who was to carry the basket, all the way up the makeshift grassy aisle. When they reached the waiting groom, the flowergirl suddenly remembered and tipped the basket of petals in a large heap all over his feet. "It was a very fragrant ceremony," recalled our bride drily.

Never be wary of bribers bearing chocolates, be they photographers or anxious mothers, as long as it doesn't get out of hand. One American bride had a clutch of tots preceding her up the aisle – and in front of them, a mother crawling backwards on her hands and knees, offering candy in one outstretched hand.

Another of our weddings saw a small flowergirl who thought she was supposed to throw her flowers in people's faces. As the guests caught on, they covered up before the little petal-pelter, cringing away as she advanced up the aisle.

At a traditional Sudanese wedding, don't forget your matches. It is the job of the maid of honour to burn seven broomsticks, to symbolize the discarding of bad habits before starting married life.

Right up there in our Hall of Shame is the 7-year-old bridesmaid who mooned the entire congregation halfway through the service, at which point it was discovered that she had managed to rid herself of her knickers on the way to the church. "She doesn't like clothes," was her mother's only defence.

The old adage that "Thrice a bridesmaid, never a bride," can be broken by being a bridesmaid seven times.

At a wedding in Sydney, the ceremony was disrupted throughout by not one but two squawking bridesmaids. When the priest reached the part when he explained, in suitably loud and sonorous tones, that marriage was for the procreation of children, the bridegroom said, (loud enough for the congregation to hear), "Oh God, does it absolutely have to be?"

In the days of yore, a bridesmaid's job didn't stop with the ceremony. At the end of the day, the bride's attendants would settle the newlyweds into bed (two's company, seventeen's a crowd?) at which point the unmarried bridesmaids would remove their stockings, stand at the end of the bed with backs turned to the couple and throw one stocking over their shoulder. If one landed on the head of one of the couple, the thrower would be the next one to marry…

"Contrary to rumour, bridesmaids are not obliged to entertain in honour of the bride,
nor to wear dresses they cannot afford."

Etiquette expert Judith Martin

– IV–

LOCATION, LOCATION, LOCATION
The still lives of the day

~

"Hire a hall: it will probably need decorating. You might find
a florist willing to hire out potted plants."
Sylvia Duncan, Getting Married, 1973

The still lives of a wedding – the church, the registry office or the site of the ceremony –
are the backdrops to the Big Day, but are often stars in their own right. In the UK, since
the legislation on where a ceremony could take place was relaxed in 1995, meaning that
thousands more venues could now be licensed, that vista has now been opened up to
include stately homes, sports stadia, train stations and anywhere deemed by the local
authority to maintain the solemnity of the occasion. Thrown into the mix is the weather,
always one of the more crucial guests at a couple's marriage, and which we have included
in this chapter as a mark of respect…

Before the Reformation, weddings were not necessarily considered a religious ceremony and,
as such, could happen anywhere. In the UK, it was not until 1754 that this was narrowed so
that marriages could only happen in Church of England churches, Jewish synagogues and
Quaker meeting rooms. This was later relaxed to include registry offices for civil ceremonies
– in Europe, each country's rules are different but usually include both a civil ceremony at a
registry, followed by a blessing in a church.

Now most commonly used as a picturesque backdrop for photographs, until the 1550s the
church porch also served as a wedding venue in its own right, the couple only then entering
the church for a final blessing. Even kings thought it normal to hover at the door: Henry III
married Eleanor of Provence in 1236 in the porch of Canterbury Cathedral. Part of the reason for
this was prosaic: the church porch was an established place for the community to witness legal
and financial transactions, so by getting married here, your congregation were your witnesses
to the details of dowry and settlement between the bride's family and the groom's…

"When doorways match and houses pair,
A marriage may be settled there."
William Scarborough, Chinese Proverbs, 1875

"It furnishes the knave with a cloak and the assassin with a dagger," wrote an 18th century moralist, but Scotland's Gretna Green is merely the most famous place for elopements. The Isle of Man also attracted abductors and elopers for a while, until its government, the Tynwald, passed an Act of startling severity: if the priest who performed a wedding ceremony was not a Manxman he "should have his ears nailed to a pillory for an hour, after which they were to be cut off and remain there, while the rest of him was to be taken back to prison."

From the Middle Ages, the Midlands was the place to get married if you liked bacon… a whole flitch of bacon was awarded to any couple who could prove that they had enjoyed absolute tranquility throughout their first year of marriage. As late as 1714, *The Spectator* reported that that year's flitch hunt had only found two success stories – a sea captain who had not seen his wife since the day of their marriage and a husband "of plain good sense and a peaceable temper" – whose wife just happened to be dumb…

One belief from ancient times was that your bride should live nearby: Greek poet Hesiod warned in c800 BC, "Be careful to marry a woman who lives near to you." Thomas Fuller, in his 1662 *Worthie Proverbs of Cheshire* was more graphic, "Better wed over the mixon than over the moor… mixon being that heap of compost which lieth in the yards of good husbands."

When ex-*Doctor Who* assistant Billie Piper married fellow thesp Laurence Fox in December 2007, they housed their reception in a series of wigwams. When one of the guests at the party was asked why he thought the couples had chosen wigwams, he shrugged. "I think it was because the Tardis was unavailable…"

Raindrops on the Big Day need not take the shine off; some adages insist that rain is actually good luck. If it rains on the wedding day itself, the bride will never need to shed tears herself, with the deluge also seen as a shower of good wishes, washing away any troubles the couple may encounter. But, to ensure good luck, a bride must be sure to keep her feet dry on her wedding day… step forward, all Sir Walter Raleighs, with your handy cloaks…

Stranger-Than-Fiction Wedding Locations:

• **During a marathon:** along the Las Vegas marathon route, couples can run through a wedding chapel to say 'I do' while jogging on the spot. In 2006, 26 couples did so... talk about marrying in haste.

• **Funeral Home:** the congregation were a little worried about too much weeping when a funeral director got married in his workplace. His bride insisted that she was "not creeped out at all"...

• **Hanging from a crane:** bride, groom and ten guests sat at chairs round a table hoisted 180 feet in the air, all in harnesses. After the ceremony, the happy couple swayed through their first dance – 'Up Where We Belong'...

• **In a bath of jelly:** two executives at the Jell-O Corporation asked their celebrant to marry them in a Boston hotel room. He found the happy couple sitting in a whirlpool bath filled with orange jelly. "We just love our work," they told him.

• **In space:** with Texan law permitting weddings where one party is absent (off the planet enough, surely), in 2003, a Russian bride in her finery was able to marry her cosmonaut fiancé while he was floating 240 miles above Houston – the first man, wearing a bow tie around his space suit, to marry in space.

• **Nudist colony:** the bridesmaids were naked, the musicians were naked, even the registrar (at the Hedonism Nudist Colony in Jamaica) was naked. The bride was most heavily dressed, in her veil, necklace and bouquet; the groom was just in his birthday suit – until he got to wear his wedding ring. Emotions were luckily the only things that rode high during the service...

• **Underwater:** "I've married people in top hats and tails. I've had brides throwing up on me and brides who have forgotten to wear waterproof makeup. One came in a weighted bridal gown, but she got snagged up on the reef and we had to cut her free." – an underwater marriage official in Florida

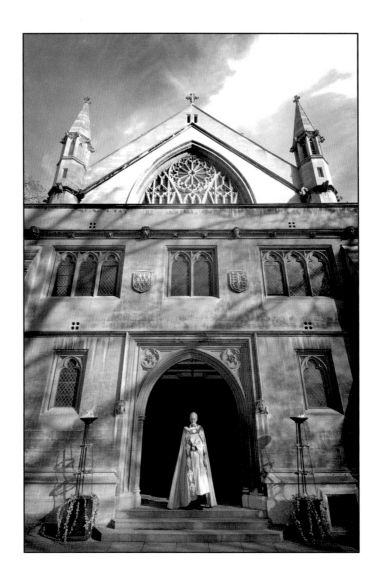

"Even a fashionable wedding, in a smart London church, affords nowadays much insight into the weaknesses of poor human nature. One sees how badly well-dressed people can behave, how they push and laugh and chatter..."

Mrs E T Cook, The Bride's Book, 1901

"A successful marriage is an edifice that must be rebuilt every day."
André Maurois (1885-1967)

Cruise weddings have been quite the rage since 1998, when a Captain Romano married a couple aboard the Grand Princess liner, the first to feature an ocean-going wedding chapel. Until then it had been a common misconception that any old ship's captain was qualified to perform weddings at sea; it's only because the Princess shipping line is subject to Bermudan law that their captains can do so – others have to be also a JP or somesuch notary.

When Queen Victoria married Prince Albert in the Royal Chapel, St James's Palace, at one in the afternoon, she once more broke with protocol. Throughout the centuries, royal weddings had been held to be too sacred for public eyes and were small, closed to anyone but family and close courtiers and, for privacy, held late in the evening or early in the morning. Not our Queen Vic. Despite the bucketing rain, her public lined the streets; 300 guests witnessed the wedding and details of her wedding attire were published in the newspapers.

Two New Yorkers enjoy marrying each other so much that they have repeated their marriage vows 55 times – and in a different location each time. They've completed their roster of every state in the US and are now shopping abroad…

Now the very acme of class as a wedding location, Mayfair wasn't always so respectable. In 18th century London, it was famous for Parson Keith's little chapel – slogan, "Happy's the wooing that's not long a-doing" – where, it was rumoured, he performed over 6,000 weddings in a self-consecrated "country-style church", (complete with porch), before party-pooper Lord Hardwycke shut him down with his Marriage Act of 1754.

Las Vegas has become synonymous with the quickie marriage and classic all-kitsch, no fuss location – and no wedding nook is more famous than the Little White Wedding Chapel, a 24-hour, 10-minister-strong business which has married off more than 800,000 people including the quickest celeb marriage of them all: the nuptials of Britney Spears and her childhood friend Jason Alexander, annulled less than 48 hours later. For those who don't even want to leave their car, there is always the Famous Tunnel of Vows Drive-Thru Wedding Chapel, an offshoot from the LWWC.

–V–

LIKE A HORSE AND CARRIAGE
Get me to the church on time

~

Marriage is not a race; you can always get there on time.
Russian proverb

The passage of true love never runs less smooth than on the way to the wedding itself. Getting to the church on time is one of the mythical tripping points of the Big Day so this could be called The Panic Chapter. But we didn't want to alarm you... ease your own blood pressure by sitting back and sharing the trials and tribulations of brides past, present and future...

Even a bride getting married at home must leave by the front door before the ceremony, otherwise she will never feel fully married. On entering and leaving the church, a bride must step over the church sill with her right foot first for both luck and happiness. At the altar itself, she should try to see that her right foot is placed ahead of the groom's – thereby ensuring her future influence over him. No-one tell the groom, otherwise there might be unseemly jostling at the altar...

When an Ancient Roman bride first arrived at the groom's house (where the ceremony was to be held), she had to smear fat on the door posts. No, not an indication of her cooking skills but a promise of her future fertility...

King George III was riding to a royal wedding when his horse suddenly reared up against a biting dog. A boy rushed out from the crowd, calmed the horse so that the king was able to regain control, then disappeared. Later, when the wedding was over and the King wanted to thank his mystery saviour, all that he could discover was that the boy was a chimney sweep – so he decreed that all chimney sweeps should be considered as lucky – leading to later Victorian and Edwardian brides even hiring sweeps to cross their path on the way to the church.

"One doesn't have to get anywhere in a marriage. It's not a public conveyance."
Iris Murdoch, A Severed Head, 1961

"The bride's father is of necessity obliged to have carriages in readiness to meet guests at the railway station, to convey them to the church and afterwards to the reception, and again to the railroad station; and this arrangement need not be mentioned in the invitations."

Emily Holt, Encyclopaedia of Etiquette, 1901

Jordan's journey to the aisle was the stuff of tabloid legend. She was shrouded by pink satin, to deter non-*OK!* readers from sneaking a peek, in a Cinderella-style carriage pulled by six white horses – who promptly drove into a ditch beside the drive up to Highclere House when they were startled by the buzzing paparazzi helicopters ahead. As the bride and her stepfather clutched each other with laughter, they were soon back on track: on arrival, a dozen white doves were released – the romantic equivalent of the relieved mobile phone call to say that all was well and the bride was here…

"In some queer test of her virginity, a bride who leaps over a rope or stool at the church gate will leave all her pets and humours behind her." – M. Radford, *Encyclopedia of Superstitions*. Does that mean Harry the Hamster gets it? Or by 'pets' are we meant to understand 'hissy fits'?

"The bride must be led to church between boys with bride laces and rosemary tied about their silken sleeves else the marriage be not a happy one" – *A Woman Killed with Kindness* – a play by Thomas Heywood 1607 which, some say, led to the custom of white ribbons ornamenting the bridal car.

'Barring the way' is an old custom from the Borders and North of England, whereby the village children prevent the couple from leaving the church until the groom has paid a 'toll', i.e. chucked them a handful of coins.

At a traditional Jewish wedding, just before the ceremony starts, the groom comes out of the synagogue to meet the bride privately and 'bedeck' her – she arrives with her veil back and it is the groom's job to bring the veil forward over her eyes so that she is obscured from the rest of the gathering… back in the days of arranged marriages, this was often the first time the bride and groom would have clapped eyes on each other.

It was nearly a Lady Godiva moment – except for the fact that the Lady wasn't naked but wearing a £23,000 white satin Versace wedding dress that took seamstresses 45 days to create. The Lady was Trudie Styler and she arrived at the 11th century Wiltshire church on horseback, draped over the withers of a white (and amiable) horse – both were later led to the reception by her more pedestrian groom: Sting.

In West Bengal, the bride is not allowed to see her mother at the time of departure from her house – one of our brides would agree with that, given that the last thing her mother did, before she left for church with the advance party, was to look at the bride and her sister, the chief bridesmaid, and say, "Oh dear, your sister looks much better than you do. Ah well, never mind."

Should a bridegroom ride to church on a mare, daughters will be born but no sons.
Welsh adage

Sandra Bullock pursued the red theme when it came to arriving at her wedding to biker boy Jesse James. Hotfoot from making the groom's wedding ring and slipping on her cowboy boots under her classic white wedding dress, Sandra climbed into a giant monster red truck for the drive to the ceremony: hope she didn't Speed….

When one of our bride's mothers called at the last minute to say that the bride was unavoidably detained for half an hour, the ushers, bridesmaids and most of the guests simply repaired to the pub next door. Trouble was, no-one thought to tell the groom, with the result that he was found at the altar, 20 minutes later, gibbering with fear that no-one had turned up because his bride had called it off.

For one couple, attempting to get to the church on time was only one of their worries in the 24 hours before the wedding. The bride spent the eve of the wedding in casualty with the couple's feverish nine-month-old daughter; next morning, the Jaguar they'd booked to take her to church was involved in a car crash on the way to pick her up. The best man, in attempting to sort this out, then disappeared, so they had to draft in a substitute. On final arrival at the church, the bride learned that the vicar, who had been called in after their original choice went on holiday, was ill and bedridden. They found a replacement at a nearby church, whereupon the bride herself went to collect him. Halfway through the service, the groom fainted and had to be revived in the vestry before the ceremony continued… "I was overcome by the stress," he said later, "but it was all worth it in the end."

When Archduchess Marie Antoinette of Austria married the young Dauphin of France who was later to become Louis XVI, she did so by proxy in Vienna, only meeting her bridegroom a month later. The journey to meet her new husband consisted of 57 carriages and a bizarre ritual at the border of France, on an island in the Rhine, where 15-year-old Marie Antoinette was made to strip naked and step into her new country, literally, with no vestige of her former life.

"Can you go a bit faster? He's beginning to sober up?" It's not just the chauffeur that needs to put his foot down; this was a bride urging the vicar to speed up the ceremony.

In Wales, *melltith* (meaning curse) is the 200 year old tradition of causing havoc for a bride and groom on their wedding day by placing obstacles in the path of the groom and forcing him to prove that he is worthy of his bride. What this means in modern terms generally includes chopping down trees – or telegraph poles – to block roads, emptying a barn of hay and piling it up at the entrance to the wedding, adding gravy browning to the water supply (guaranteed to improve that pre-wedding bath) or putting sheep in the church the night before the wedding. The last happened to a recent Welsh bride: the wedding entourage thought it very diverting but the florist was less than amused: all his creations were neatly nibbled off to just above sheep's teeth height…

Melltith Moments: Some Of Our Brides' Other Hurdles To Getting Hitched:

• **Technology:** at one American wedding, the bride, father and all bridesmaids got stuck in the lift down from their hotel suite for over two hours – with no mobiles or means of contacting the church.

• **Mechanical failure:** if you're going to get a snazzy classic car for arriving at the church, you might want a fall-back plan. One bride had hired Elton John's old Rolls Royce, sky blue and covered in clouds, with matchingly clad chauffeur. With two minutes to go – and 15 minutes' drive from the ceremony – she found out that it had broken down and had to wedge herself into her sister's tiny Fiat Panda: difficult with the vast, crinolined hoop skirt and Vivienne Westwood corset that she had chosen. Onlookers snickered as the Panda drove off, the bride totally hidden by frills.

• **Map-reading mistakes:** when our bride got to the church on the hottest day of the year, the entourage's minibus, stuffed to the gills with bridesmaids large and small, had disappeared without trace in the 500 yards of apparent Bermuda Triangle between house and church: the minibus driver had shot straight past the church. By the time, he had realised his mistake and turned around, the overheated congregation had actually left the church and the bride, still waiting and baking back outside the church, was staving off a nervous breakdown.

• **Domineering fathers:** one of our brides got to the church on time but then sat in the car for an hour, trapped there by her father trying to talk her out of marrying the groom. Eventually the vicar tapped on the window to say that there was another wedding booked in half an hour, so if they didn't get on with it, the wedding would have to be cancelled. Next minute, the bride had flown out of the car and was rushing up the aisle. The service went ahead at top speed and without any of the hymns; when they came out, the next bridal party was already waiting to go in. Romance was only just alive…

"Going to a friend's wedding for me is basically like going to a friend's funeral: after each one, you never get your friend back."

Overheard at one of our weddings, from a world-weary bridesmaid
who was clearly tired of her job description.

I'm getting married in the morning,
Ding! Dong! The bells are gonna chime.
Pull out the stopper;
Let's have a whopper;
But get me to the church on time!"
1956 song from My Fair Lady

When the Sultan of Brunei's son was married, there were no novelty tuk-tuks or pony-and-trap, but one contender for Most Vulgar Wedding Car Ever: a £10million golden-encrusted stretch Rolls Royce, with a specially adapted open-topped rear with a double throne for the 30 year old Crown Prince and his bride Sarah Salleh, aged 17, topped off by a vast golden umbrella. Even money can't buy off the weather…

One of our brides was also keen on the golden Rolls-Royce idea – and bought a gold-coloured one for her husband as a surprise, meaning to present it to him as their going-away vehicle. But he saw it parked outside the reception and, thinking it belonged to one of their guests, remarked to his new wife, "Who could possibly have come in that hideously tacky motor?" Sad to say, they are now divorced…

Bad weather on the way to the wedding is believed to signify unhappiness in the marriage – although cloudy skies and wind will merely result in a stormy partnership – while snow on the way is a harbinger of fertility and prosperity.

Stella McCartney and groom Alasdhair Wills made the short journey from church to reception on the neo-gothic estate of Mount Stuart, in a carriage pulled by Clydesdale carthorses. Famous for their soup plate hooves and vast iron shoes, such footwear and size might have come in handy for the fash pack that had to pick their way down a muddy lane in their highest Manolos. Ah, the heart bleeds.

In America, we are told, bell-ringing is substituted by motorists continually blowing their horn if they pass a wedding or wedding retinue. This wasn't known by the Hungarian-born chauffeur driving one of our American brides to the church, who thought that the constant klaxons were in protest at his large limo blocking the traffic. So she was horrified when he got out of the limo and started a punch-up with another driver… though he was good enough to get back in, limping slightly and bleeding from the nose, to drive her the rest of the way – without a word said.

The pealing of bells at a wedding marks the start of the 'getting there' period and was done, initially by the pagan Ancient Britons, to drive away the evil spirits that were assumed to hang around waiting to ruin a bride's day. As with so many other pagan beliefs, this precaution was discreetly absorbed into the ritual of the early Christian church and bell-ringing is now more associated with announcement.

Though the bridal car is an integral part of the wedding day, it's not usually part of the wedding party itself... but when one Tennessee groom was jilted by his fiancée, he decided he would marry his one true love, his 1996 Mustang GT, before having his hopes crashed again. It was after he listed his new fiancée's birthplace as Detroit, her father as 'Henry Ford' and her blood type as '10-W-40' that the courtroom clerk began to suspect that 'she' was just a vehicle for his marital desires. "In California, they are doing same-sex marriages," said the would-be groom, "so why can't we do the good ole boy thing and marry our cars and trucks?" Perhaps he needs to get together with the woman who married the Berlin Wall...

Grace Kelly's new mother-in-law brought a lover to her son Prince Rainier's wedding, posing as a chauffeur. He actually turned out to be a notorious jewel thief, 'René the Cane', who robbed wedding guests of over $60,000 of jewellery.

"*Wedlock's a lane where there is no turning.*"
Dinah Craik, Magnus and Morna, 1860

–VI–

THE CAST LIST
Father of bride, mothers-in-law, pets. And baby comes too!

~

"The business of Mrs. Bennet's life [is] to get her daughters married."
Pride & Prejudice, Jane Austen, 1813

The *dramatis personae* of a wedding could sell out a West End theatre any night of the week. Fathers of the bride who attempt to bribe their daughters not to marry the groom; mothers-in-law who would rather hurl some crumbs in their son's new wife's face than give her a welcoming smile; dogs who fancy themselves as the best man and the babies who do their level gurgling best to steal the limelight from their marrying mums and dads… it is truly the rich tapestry of life, stitched tightly into a small frame: the wedding day.

From the in-laws' feast in Ancient Greece to the knees-up in the Middle Ages, what we now call the rehearsal dinner – where both families mingle the night before the Big Day – became an occasion for endless toasts and clinking of glasses. This was to scare away the devil and evil spirits, who loved to spoil weddings but were obviously fragile little flowers who couldn't cope with a spot of noise: especially noise – clink, clink - that sounded a little like the ringing of church bells.

"Father always wanted to be the corpse at every funeral, the bride at every wedding and the baby at every christening," – daughter Alice Lee Roosevelt was brooking no limelight-stealing by her father President Theodore Roosevelt at her 1906 wedding.

"To my mind, a wedding's a very poor play. There are only two parts in it – the bride and bridegroom. The best man is only a walk-on gentleman. With the exception of a crying father, and a snivelling mother, the rest are supers who have to dress well and have to pay for their insignificant parts in the shape of costly presents." – the Cockney clerk in *Diary of a Nobody*, by George & Weedon Grossmith.

"An expert photographer can make the happy couple look like film stars... it's wonderful watching the bride's father, a few years later, idly flicking through the album of photos, the tears gently rolling down his cheeks... as he remembers what the whole day cost him."

Duffer's Guide to Getting Married, 1986

*"Enjoy the little things, for one day you may look back
and realise they were the big things."*
Writer Robert Brault

"Behind every successful man is a surprised mother-in-law..."
Anon

"I knew a mother who deliberately drugged herself to appear ill on the day of the wedding, because she thought her 'sickness' might stop her daughter marrying a man whom she did not like." – Sylvia Duncan, *How To Be a Better Wife*, 1956

No wedding entourage would be complete without the celebrant, be he or she a vicar, a rabbi or a civil registrar. We have heard legion tales of drunken vicars, fire-and-brimstone priests, a rabbi who sent the wedding party to sleep with his chanting. But our favourite anecdote concerns the vicar who concluded at the end of the ceremony, "And I may now kiss the bride – " and lunged forward, catching the bride by surprise and sweeping her into a full-blown snog. It turned out later that he was an old friend of the bride's who had always held a candle for her but had left it too late to declare himself in a more conventional or well-timed way. Luckily, the groom was prepared to take a relaxed view…

There was a difficult moment at one wedding when, at the crucial juncture of the ceremony, the best man began to fumble in his pockets for the wedding rings. When the bride and groom started to get visibly alarmed – and the 100 guests held their breath – the best man decided to put them out of their misery. He turned and whistled loudly, whereupon all heads turned to see the couple's two small pooches proudly walking down the aisle, with tiny pillows holding a ring each tied to their backs with white ribbons – the canine equivalent of the ringbearer's cushion.

Weddings – and who's invited – can often be a recipe for serious family feuds. When Nadia Sawalha sold the trashy mag rights to her wedding of 2002, her more famous sister Julia Sawalha (of Saffy in *AbFab* fame) and her actor boyfriend Alan Davies had the hissy fit of the decade about such an invasion of privacy. The hitherto close sisters didn't talk again until Julia split with the notoriously reclusive Davies in 2004, two years later…

Best friend, best man – a dog can be all things for all people: like the bride that was actually walked up the aisle by her own lurcher… had the father of the bride been confined to kennels? But some couples are surprised to find that old Fido has no actual authority. Charolette Richards, the minister and owner of famous Las Vegas wedding spot, the Little White Wedding Chapel, has seen 'em all (even 'marrying' a female great dane and a male pug in London in 2005). "One couple took me to the Grand Canyon to get married above it in a helicopter and they wanted their dog to be their witness. I said, 'A dog doesn't understand what's going on, the pilot has to be your witness,' and they said, 'We want the dog.' So I said, 'That's okay, we'll put his pawprint on your licence, but he's not going to be your witness…'"

"All women become like their mothers. That is their tragedy. No man does. That's his."
Oscar Wilde (1854-1900)

Out of the 2,500 that came to Prince Charles's wedding to Lady Diana Spencer, Diana was allowed to choose 100 guests, her parents 50 each – while the Queen worried about which of her 2,000 closest friends to invite…

Don't alert the media, but some celebrities don't actually want the whole cast list and accompanying paparazzi. When Gwyneth Paltrow married Coldplay singer Chris Martin in 2003, they opted for a secret quickie ceremony in California with the smallest possible guestlist: not even family members were present. Oscar-winner Kate Winslet married Sam Mendes in the Caribbean, with just Mia, Kate's toddler daughter, present. When Fern Britton married her second husband, chef Phil Vickery, they just drove themselves to their local registry office and plucked two witnesses from the street. "I couldn't have given two hoots about the lack of wedding party," Fern said later, "It was a very happy, romantic and intimate occasion."

"Most of us have one or two unspeakably awful relatives, but we've had our entire lives to get used to them. And most of us voluntarily chose our spouses, so we've only got ourselves to blame. But with our children's in-laws, we're suddenly shunted into close proximity with two people with whom we've nothing in common except that our kid took a shine to their kid…" – Mark Steyn, *The Spectator*, 2004

Overheard being said by one father of the bride to his wife at their daughter's wedding reception, "Look on the bright side – we're not losing a daughter, we're gaining a bathroom…"

For some mothers of the bride, their daughter's wedding is a taxing drain on their own self-esteem. "Whatever I tried on, I felt insecure about," said one. In the end, she opted for a safe-but-classic suit in amethyst blue, only to come face-to-face on the Big Day with the mother of the groom, who was squeezed into a black leather minidress, skyscraper scarlet Christian Louboutins and skintight red leather gloves. "I was torn between relief because she was so inappropriate, horror that this vamp was going to be my poor daughter's mother-in-law or just plain jealousy because she looked like pure sex and there I was, a pale and uninteresting Virgin Mary type – so I just stared at her open-mouthed until she said, 'What? Do I have something in my teeth?'"

At a Sikh wedding, the two fathers of bride and groom exchange money, rings and – thank the lord for anti-dandruff shampoos – even turbans…

Two cannibals comparing marital experiences. One cannibal, "I don't really like my mother-in-law." The other: "Don't bother with her, then, just eat the chips."

And Baby Comes Too!

• **Madonna and Guy Ritchie:** the only part of the Scottish wedding weekend that wasn't under wraps was the christening of young Rocco Ritchie, two days before the wedding ceremony, when he was just four months old.

• **Michael Douglas and Catherine Zeta Jones:** at three months old, baby Dylan was the youngest of four generations of Joneses at the couple's New York wedding. 85-year-old gran Zeta wept with joy throughout, but Dylan, in a blue pinstriped romper suit (going for a banker-cum-burper look) was wide-eyed and silent…

• **Posh and Becks:** even 4-month-old baby Brooklyn had to wear a security tag to deter gate-crashers – but he was presumably cheered up by his £2,500 fancy duds: a purple suit and purple cowboy hat specially designed for him by Antonio Berardi.

• **TomKat:** seven-month-old Suri Cruise stole the show when she arrived at the Italy-based wedding in her mother's arms, showing her budding fashionista pedigree in a white silk shift and then chewing on her dad's Armani-clad shoulder.

Sir Alan Sugar may be the big bad wolf of industry nowadays but back when he married his loyal wife Ann, he was a mere *Apprentice* in the eyes of the father of the bride. At a party for their ruby wedding anniversary, Sugar recounted a secret about his wife's father during a conversation about how long they had been married. "So she said to me, 'Do I see a tear in your eyes? Don't tell me you're feeling sentimental.' I said, "Forty years ago, your father took out his old army pistol, held it to my head and told me if I didn't marry you he would make sure I was banged up in jail for 40 years. So, yeah, I am being sentimental – the thing is, I would be getting out tomorrow…'"

Sometimes the bit players of the Big Day inadvertently find themselves centre-stage for all the wrong reasons. Like the father of the bride who, estranged from his wife, seduced one of the bride's racier friends – or the supposedly celibate priest who slept with the bride's sister after a boozy wedding reception… forever ruining the deeply Catholic bride's view of her own nuptials, though her sister was obviously not so religiously bothered.

One bride had always dreamed of her father walking her up the aisle but he died eight months before the Big Day. So her family came up with a novel solution – and had his ashes transformed into a graphite 'blue diamond' for the bride to carry in a pouch with her bouquet. "I held on to her left hand and she carried her father in her right." He was truly our diamond geezer."

One of our grooms found out at least two years after his wedding that the reason his bride had been late to the church was that her father had spent half an hour trying to persuade her not to marry him, at one point offering her £50,000 not to go through with the wedding.

In an ancient Welsh custom, the bride's father poses a series of riddles to the hapless groom while he's waiting for the bride to arrive. Traditionally, there are no hints given…

In some Pakistani villages, it's even worse: the groom is taken before the relatives of the bride, who then insult him with every curse and damning opinion that they can think of while he must remain silent; the theory being that if he can take this treatment, he has nothing to fear from what his bride might say in times to come…

King Ethelred the Unready (968-1016) spent his wedding night in bed with his wife… and his new mother-in-law.

"An unhappy alternative is before you, Elizabeth. From this day you must be a stranger to one of your parents. Your mother will never see you again if you do not marry Mr. Collins, and I will never see you again if you do." – Mr Bennet advises Lizzie not to marry oily Mr Collins, *Pride & Prejudice*, Jane Austen, 1813

A minister remembered how, at one of his earlier weddings, he was very late: causing huge anxiety in the bridal couple. Years later, he met the husband again by chance and said, "Do you remember that awful fright I gave you on your wedding day?" "I do indeed," replied the man. "She's still with me."

−VII−

USHERS TO USHER
Jobs for the boys

༄

"I prefer men in uniform. They're used to taking orders."
Anon

Historically, brides were more often captured or purchased than wooed – and this was where the groomsmen came into their own. One weedy Lochinvar turning up and slinging your daughter over the back of his pony wasn't too much of a threat – but Lochinvar and his Lusty Lads were a different prospect and harder to argue with. Nowadays, the legacy of bride capture lives on in the body of men who surround the groom on his big day, whether you call them groomsmen or ushers. The best man himself is like Ronseal, he does what it says on the tin and is the rock of all ages all day – although we sympathise with one of our best men who said plaintively in his speech: "If I'm the best man, how come the bride isn't with me?!"

"He is the necessary ark of safety to this agitated groom. He accompanies him to church, he follows him to the altar, he sees to it that he has the ring in his pocket, he stands at his right hand, a little behind him, during the ceremony, he attends to all his small wants, holds his hat. Then in a coupé all alone by himself, the best man follows the young couple home." – M.E.W. Sherwood, *Correct Social Usage*, 1903

In the bad old days, being an usher wasn't just a case of guiding Aunt Beryl to her seat in the church but more about being the groom's partner in crime, aiding him in his bride-capture, with the "best man" being the strongest warrior, fighting off anyone trying to save the hapless damsel. At the wedding, the groom's men would dress identically to the groom to confuse anyone from the bride's family who had come to take their revenge on the would-be husband. Afterwards, the best man would act as go-between, soothing the bride's family and arranging for a bride price after the fact.

"That is what marriage really means: helping one another to reach the full status of being persons; responsible and autonomous beings who do not run away from life."

Paul Tournier (1898-1986)

"I pay very little regard... to what any young person says on the subject of marriage. If they profess a disinclination for it, I only set it down that they have not yet seen the right person."

Jane Austen, Mansfield Park, 1814

*"Friendship is born at that moment when one person says to another,
'What! You too? I thought I was the only one.'"*

C. S. Lewis (1898 - 1963)

To this day, some cultures still have mock kidnap as part of the nuptial tradition: like in Germany, where it's known as *Brautentführung*. The best man spirits the bride away after the wedding ceremony to a secret place like a woodland clearing or a bar, where the game is to drink as much champagne as possible until the groom finds them. The longer he takes to find them , the higher the bill that he must pay…

A sex-starved Romulus, the founder of Rome, took bride-capture to extremes: he and his friends captured (and raped) 700 women from the next door Sabine tribe. By the time the Sabine menfolk really got their act together, the Sabine women had already started producing Roman babies so, eminently sensible as women are in these circumstances, they married their Roman capturers and persuaded both sides to lay down weapons and live together.

The bride price is a cultural staple throughout the world, paid by the groom and usually negotiated by his entourage as a token of the groom's appreciation for his bride and as recompense to the family for its loss, paid in cash, gold or services (labours of love). In Asia, the price is often still delicately wheedled out through matchmakers while in Africa, families meet up and thrash it out directly.

In the 17th century, morning weddings were increasingly avoided for the reason that the bridegroom and his escorts were apt to appear "unshaven and wearing dirty or negligent attire", either because they had come straight from early-morning labours, or because of a last round of all-night-partying the night before.

Ushers are hard-wired to spring into action when disaster looms, ready to save the day. One of our grooms had forgotten the ring so sent an usher (a female one, unusually) back to his house to fetch it. The usherette went into the house and got the ring, but set off the burglar alarm. Panicking, she bolted from the house, slamming the door behind her, clutching the ring - but leaving the car keys and house keys in the locked house behind her. Unable to get a cab, she ended up flagging down a fire-engine, arriving at the wedding in true style… though a little red-faced.

World champion best man is surely Ting Ming Siong, from Malaysia, who has been best man no fewer than 465 times. Groom No. 466 may want him to re-jig the speech a little.

Back in the mists of time, the groom's wedding retinue would wear floral 'favours' in courtly respect for the bride, dating back to the days when a lady at a jousting tournament would show her 'favour' of a particular knight by giving him some flower or scarf to wear tucked into his armour. These eventually evolved into the buttonholes of today.

–VIII–

DEARLY BELOVED
The ceremony itself

~

*"Any marriage ceremony where the bride is allowed to speak and
wear clothes is doomed to failure."*
Quark from Star Trek: DS9

In all the fuss about ushers' breakfasts, seating plans and the need for Great Aunt Muriel to be given no champagne on account of her drink problem, the marriage itself can often take a back seat. But the ceremony is the very heart and soul of the day: everyone else may have come for the party but you have come here to get married, be it with pomp and circumstance in the eyes of the Lord – or on a hillside, singing your vows to each other. Every wedding ceremony is different. The preconception is that if you've heard one 'Dearly Beloved, we are gathered here…", you've heard them all. The misconception is that you need to make yours different, just for the sake of it. If you want the 'sounding brass' reading, O Love Divine and a flock of silver-buckled pageboys, then it's your day. If you want to get hitched in a white sarong on a Barbados beach, by a registrar whose second job is serving you your croissants at the hotel buffet, then go wild. Just don't panic.

Until 1885, marriages only took place between 8am and 12 noon because they had to be followed by mass – and fasting prior to mass was essential. During one post-nuptial Mass, the Catholic priest dropped the Communion wafer down the bride's front and, before she could stop him, dived into her cleavage to fish it out again… perhaps the fasting had gone to his head.

In the 14th century, in a wedding ceremony reported in Richard II's reign, a woman had to promise to be "bonlich and buxom in bed" – with 'obey' in the marriage ceremony turning out to be more to do with allowing conjugal rights than the usual obedience and assenting. Diana, Princess of Wales, was the first Royal to omit 'obey' when she married Princes Charles in 1981.

Vicar: 'Wilt thou have this woman. . .?'
Bridegroom: 'I wilt.'

As she hears the wedding march, a nervous bride can only focus on three things she has to direct herself towards: aisle, altar, hymn, or, as the congregation hears her muttering, "I'll alter him!"

Anon

The phrase 'given away' used to be rather more literal than it is today. In the Old Testament, Leah's father offers to give her away to Jacob, in return for seven years' work – and the view that women were a chattel to be traded persisted for centuries. As late as 1832, a Cumberland farmer sold his wife in Carlisle for 20 shillings and a Newfoundland dog.

A pageboy was following one of our brides up the aisle, when he spotted a mouse running up ahead of her. Jumping up and down and pointing at the terrified rodent. he squealed excitedly "Kill him, Daddy, kill him!" Unfortunately, most of the congregation just saw him pointing up the aisle, apparently exhorting his dad to kill…the hapless groom.

Almost all of what we now consider to be 'traditional' wedding music is 19th century in origin… the vast majority of which was not originally composed for weddings but came into vogue once it had been played at the many weddings of Queen Victoria's children and grandchildren.

When asked by a Warwickshire vicar why they had chosen the hymn, "Sheep may safely graze," for their wedding, the bride replied that it was because they were both vegetarians…

At one wedding, when the groom knelt down, written across the soles of his shoes by the ushers, and now on show to the congregation, were the letters "HE-" and "-LP". The priest was not amused by the shouts of laughter at the most devout part of the ceremony – and the groom was still none the wiser.

It was the fraught moment in any wedding ceremony when everyone holds their breath at the priest's dutiful enquiry as to anyone knowing of any reason why the bride and groom should not be wed – when suddenly, a clear, piping voice rang out, "YES! I know why they shouldn't get married." Gasps and bated breaths all around the church. On went the voice, "SHE CAN'T COOK!" It was the bride's much younger brother – who had clearly had about as many burnt fishfingers at the hands of his dozy, lovelorn sister as he could take…

Why is a wedding ring worn on the third finger? The ancient Egyptians believed that a vein of blood – called *veni amori*, the vein of love - ran directly from the third finger on the left hand right up to the heart.

"This is the stuff of which fairy tales are made." – Archbishop of Canterbury, Robert Runcie, 1981, on the wedding of Princes Charles and Diana Spencer, little knowing the Brothers Grimm days that lay ahead for the couple.

"*Happy marriages begin when we marry the ones we love, and they blossom when we love the ones we marry.*"

Author Tom Mullen

"The bridal kiss originated when the first male reptile licked the first female reptile, implying in a subtle, complimentary way that she was as succulent as the small reptile he had for dinner the night before. "

F. Scott Fitzgerald (1896-1940)

Many couples prefer the old order of service where the vicar introduces the sacrament of marriage as 'an honourable estate, instituted of God…not to be enterprised or taken in hand unadvisedly, lightly or wantonly,' but few know that it then goes on, 'to satisfy men's carnal lusts and appetites, like brute beasts that have no understanding'. Strangely enough, most vicars are happy to leave that part out…

"She takes it by tradition from her Fellow-Gossips, that she must weep shoures upon her Marriage Day: though by the vertue of mustarde and onyons, if she cannot naturally bring them forth." – *The Year Book*, William Hone, 1827

Cheryl Cole, with her tiny waist and doll-like figure, has admitted that she wanted to include "for fatter or thinner" in the marriage vows – but that husband Ashley Cole put his foot down.

At a Quaker wedding, where worship is mostly silent with the occasional interjection or reflection from one of the Friends, the marriage ceremony might be entirely silent except for the couple's vows. With no priest, they effectively marry themselves, with the rest of the congregation as their witnesses: all present sign the wedding certificate.

Elvis Presley's long-awaited marriage ceremony to Priscilla Beaulieu in 1967 took only eight minutes at the Aladdin Hotel in Las Vegas. When a newsman commented to a photographer, "Snap him [Elvis] smiling. He doesn't smile much lately," Presley joked, "How can I look happy when I'm scared?" He then looked over at his father, laughed and yelped, "Daddy, help!" Elvis's father shook his head and said, "Can't do it, son. You're on your own."

Calling All Tossers: A Few Flakes Of Confetti History

• In Elizabethan times, brides were showered with symbols of the groom's trade – so a blacksmith's bride flinched before nails and a tailor's bride smiled gratefully as scraps of cloth fluttered past her. Well, it was better than a slap in the face with a wet fish – oh, sorry, Mrs Fishmonger – but bummer if your husband's a butcher…

• Meanwhile, in Italy and other European countries, they were becoming a little more exotic: the word confetti is Italian for sweets, or confectionery, originally nuts and small fruits, nowadays usually interpreted as sugared almonds.

• Paper confetti – now no longer allowed by many churches within church grounds – is a modern invention. A scientific magazine in 1895 first recorded the 'throwing of confetti' as being the 'renaissance of French gayety' at the cabaret hotspot Le Casino de Paris. It soon took off and by 1900, machinery had been created to manufacture up to 3,300 lbs of confetti per day… One collector, in California, owns a record-breaking 1,700 unique shapes.

The ultimate soap wedding is clearly going to be an emotive prize but we plump for That Wedding (one of 35 before and since) on *Neighbours* – as Scott and Charlene tied the knot. Not only was it given an extra frisson because of the real life romance between Jason Donovan and Kylie Minogue, but it was a phenomenal success for *Neighbours*. The episode, first aired in July 1987, sent ratings through the roof, and even made the cover of *TIME* Australia, with thousands of fans gathering for a re-enactment of the cake-cutting at a Sydney shopping centre on the day the wedding aired, causing high emotion and some fans to even faint…

Someone Else Doing The Hard Work: Our Top Ten Readings

Tread softly, for you tread on my dreams – *Cloths of Heaven*, W B Yeats
Sounding brass and a clanging cymbal – I Corinthians 13:1-13
Rise up, my love, my fair one, and come away – Song of Solomon or the Song of Songs
Once you are Real you can't be ugly – *The Velveteen Rabbit*, Margery Williams
My true love hath my heart – *The Bargain*, Sir Philip Sydney
Love one another but make not a bond of love – *The Prophet*, Khalil Gibran
Love is not love which alters – *Sonnet 116*, William Shakespeare
"Hope" is the thing with feathers – Emily Dickenson
Go Placidly – *Desiderata*
How do I love thee? Let me count the ways? – *Sonnets from the Portuguese*, Elizabeth Barrett Browning

Never let this urban myth go cold. One couple supposedly met with the village church organist to discuss their music. "To come out, please can we have the theme tune to the 'Robin Hood' film?" asked the bride. She meant, of course, the over-used Bryan Adams ballad, 'Everything I Do, I Do It For You', so she was surprised on the day by the organist bursting into the rousing strains of 'Robin Hood, Robin Hood, riding through the Glen'…

The way to a man's heart isn't always through his stomach. The Berber women of North Africa say to their men during a wedding ceremony, "You have captured my liver," that organ rather than the heart being the seat of love. Hence their expression of ultimate adoration: "I love you with all my liver!"

One of our brides made it through the ceremony without a hitch, but was distracted towards the end by the thought of how she was going to sit sidesaddle pillion on the Vespa they were using to get to the reception. Suddenly she saw their vicar raising his hand and, losing her sanity for a moment, thought he was giving her a high-five of congratulations and hurriedly slapped him right back. Of course he was actually just giving the newlyweds the final blessing.

"Smile! It flatters your husband."
Fanny Fern, 19th century American columnist (1811-72)

"I wonder, by my troth, what you and I did, before we lov'd?"
John Donne (1572-1631)

–IX–

CANAPÉ NOW OR CANAPÉ LATER?
Feeding the hordes at the reception

∼

"Wedlock, indeed, hath oft compared been to public feasts, where meet a public rout
Where they that are without would fain go in and they that are within would fain go out."
Sir John Davies (1569-1626)

All the pressure is off, the tears have flowed, the right people turned up at the right time, the vows are made and the church door has clanged securely behind the departing newlyweds: so the emotional jumping through of hoops is over, right? Wrong. The reception is just the second stage of the marathon: you've turned for home but the road is just as rocky… we have the hurdles of speech-making, eating canapés while juggling champagne glass, handbag and smalltalk repertoire, cake-cutting and the art of present-giving. Not to mention the egos of the supporting entourages, the demands of your guests, that feeling the bride has that she must speak to Every Person There. But no matter how whirlwind and hectic it seems, the crucial thing to remember is that You Are Having Fun….

Little Boy: "Daddy, how much does it cost to get married?"
Father: "I don't know, son, I'm still paying for it."

"When it comes to marriage, people care only about keeping up with the times. They spend extravagantly on material things…the decorated pavilion to welcome the bride and her elegant sedan chair, the banquet where the two families meet and exchange gifts, all require the most fantastic outlays of cash – all for the sake of a single public display, ignoring the needs of the 'eight mouths' at home…" – Ch'en Hung-Mou, China, 1750s – but could have been written by a Daily Mail columnist today…

At least the English tradition is to have just one day for a wedding reception: the real party animals are from East India – where receptions once lasted 15 days – or the Hasidic Jews, who keep up the festivities for a week.

"The bridegroom is not expected to be in a state of mind to deliver a grand oration."
'Best Man', Marriage Etiquette, 1931

"Speech-making is a bit like prospecting for black gold.
If you don't strike oil in 10 minutes, stop boring."

Anon

"A wedding speech should be like a girl's dress: long enough to cover the important bits and short enough to be interesting." Anon

There was a surprising toast from the father of the bride at one of our weddings, when the proud papa made teasing reference to his feisty daughter's recent breast enlargement with the little ditty, "Mel, Mel, the Bitch from Hell, with tits made out of silicone gel"…

One of our grooms engaged mouth before brain when he said of his bride, "I think we can all agree that Philippa looks absolutely lovely… so a BIG thankyou to the makeup artist…!"

The world's most expensive wedding billed in at an eye-watering $60 million. This paid for silver-encased, 20 page invitations; a six day celebration for 1,200 of their closest friends, held at a picture perfect French chateau; and a Bollywood show featuring Kylie Minogue. The man with the deep, deep pockets was Lakshmi Mittal, the world's third richest man, and the lucky bride was his daughter, Vanisha, who luckily didn't live up to her name and turned up on time to enjoy her bargain-basement bridal bonanza.

Worried you've invited too many people to your wedding? Comfort yourself with thoughts of the world's largest wedding reception, which took place after a Jewish ceremony in Jerusalem in 1993. A full 30,000 guests were reputed to have flocked in for the reception; now that's what we call popularity. Just imagine the wedding list…

Liza Minelli and David Gest registered for 389 wedding gifts from Tiffany & Co., totalling over £130,000 – including soapdishes at £350 and a pair of candlesticks for £2,300. They did, however, give most things back when they parted company 16 months later.

In Eastern Europe, the bride is brought salt, a candle and a piece of bread as gifts: ensuring that her life will have spice, light and plenty. Put that in your Tiffany soapdish and mull awhile, Liza and David…

"Remember that weddings can be an expensive business for guests, so do not shock them by including such things as a grand piano on the present list." – Sylvia Duncan, *Getting Married*, 1973

When the Queen, then a Princess, married the Duke of Edinburgh, they received 1500 presents, including a picnic basket from her sister, Princess Margaret, a filly from the Aga Khan – and a piece of cloth crocheted by Mahatma Gandhi which old Queen Mary thought was a loincloth…

"That married couples can live together day after day is one
miracle the Vatican has overlooked."
Bill Cosby

*"I love being married; it's so great to find that one special person that
you want to annoy for the rest of your life."*
Rita Rudner

Celebrity Wedding Menus… Though We Know They Only Ate A Lettuce Leaf…

• **Britney Spears and Kevin Federline:** it was a Louisiana lard-up for our Deep Southern songstrel: chicken fingers, mashed potatoes and crab cakes. Oh, and let's not forget the cash bar – because being worth several million apparently means you can't afford to buy your friends drinks on your wedding day…

• **Charles & Diana:** oh, Eighties cuisine, you have a lot to be forgiven for. Fancy some brill in lobster sauce followed by chicken breasts stuffed with lamb mousse? No? Then pity the hundreds of Royal guests who had to feign delight at this menu…

• **Edward and Mrs Simpson:** apparently no-one saw the irony in the choice of chicken à la King as the main course of their nuptial feast

• **Elizabeth Hurley and Arun Nayar:** guests at Sudeley Castle enjoyed a medieval banquet of guinea fowl with sage and poached pears, that was modelled on the wedding feast of Henry VIII's sixth and surviving wife, Catherine Parr, a former resident of Sudeley.

• **Elton John and David Furnish:** having toyed with the idea of shepherd's pie, the final menu was roast lamb and gravy, followed by a 'tasty chocolate log'. Sometimes you couldn't make this stuff up…

A tin of chicken in jelly may not be on everyone's wedding present list but to one newly-wed couple in 1956, it was such a delicacy that they squirrelled it away to enjoy as a treat on a rainy day… cut to their golden wedding anniversary, 50 years to the day after they were first given the chicken. The aged husband, 73, sat down to tuck in to the tin of chicken, natural jelly and salt – but his wife decided that it was a little past her sell-by date.

A custom that has unaccountably died out in Russia is that of giving the bride and groom a pair of boiled bear testicles to ensure fertility…

Let them eat cake:

In Roman times, at a 'confarreatio' (the highest level of marriage, for patricians – and a possible root for the word 'confetti') the bride ate a piece of cake made from 'farr' flour and water, not just to prove that she was up to unappetising tasks but to signify the hope that the bridal couple would never lack the necessities of life.

"Bonnets are not put off at a reception. Gloves are only laid aside while one is eating."
Emily Holt, Encyclopaedia of Etiquette, 1901

The classic best man's gaffe is, apparently, "To the Bride and Gloom!" — but here are some of our real life equivalents: the best man who joked about the groom's time in rehab, when his parents hadn't even known he was an alcoholic (they walked out) or the worst best man who used his speech to inform the bride that the groom had a child by someone else... something the groom had failed to mention.

Let 'Em Eat Cake:

Under Elizabeth I, we see the advent of 'bride-cakes', richly-made square buns of sugar, eggs, milk, spices and currants. Some were tossed over the bride's head when she left the church – the rest were stacked in a high mound at a table at the feast afterwards, over which the newlyweds kissed: if they succeeded in doing so without knocking the pile over, they would lead prosperous lives together from then on.

It was in 1688, when Charles II brought French pastry chefs back from his exile, that the Glorious Revolution got a little more glorious. They took the square mound of buns and cemented them together in tiers with marzipan, icing the layers with as many sugary fripperies as time and money allowed. The story goes that one sweet genius was inspired by the silhouette of St Bride's Church in Fleet St to make his own towering creation: a shape that any of us recognize today as the classic tiered wedding cake.

By the middle of the 18th century, though the silhouette remained the same, the cakes got larger and larger, so the denser, more solid fruit cake was introduced – and the icing became exclusively white: to emphasise the bride's virginity, naturally. The richer the mix, the more the prosperity enjoyed by the couple in the future.

The world's most expensive cake – on display at a Beverly Hills Luxury Brands Bridal Show – baked in at $20 million, being stuffed with diamonds.

"In all of the wedding cake, hope is the sweetest of plums." – Douglas Jerrold, writer (1803-1857)

−X−

KICK UP YOUR HEELS!
Heading into the happily ever after

∼

A marriage may be made in heaven, but the maintenance must be done on earth.
English adage

After the cake has been cut, it's time for dancing, then all the hullaballoo that marks the departure of the bride and groom. But what then? What superstitions lurk from the first night to colour the happy couple's lives together? Which celebrities never even managed to consummate their marriages, or did so only to dissolve the marriage a matter of hours later? What insights can we give to nervous newlyweds about heading in the Happily Ever After? It's nearly the end of the Big Day and there are still all sorts of matters to ponder. This is good; life is never dull. Just hold on, grab some mane and ride with us into the sunset…

One of our would-be-brides was jilted only days before the wedding… the only good thing to come out of the tragedy was finding out about the surprise that her father had had up his sleeve for her at the reception: he had booked a troupe of Morris Dancers, bells, sticks and all…

As if the first dance weren't excruciating enough, another American tradition that has seeped into some British nuptials is the practice of 'forcing' the couple to kiss – traditionally by tapping champagne glasses with their cutlery but in more modern times with ever-more elaborate tricks and whims: like the couple who (we're depressed even writing this) installed a small putting green. The couple had to kiss whenever a guest got a hole in one…

One couple, instead of doing a first dance, did a karaoke number but got carried away into doing some ceroc on the last chorus. The bride promptly twisted both ankles and had to be carted off the dancefloor in a trailer, attached to a lawn-mower backed into the tent.

"Love flies, runs and rejoices; it is free and nothing can hold it back."
Thomas à Kempis (1380-1471)

You invite people to your wedding and, a few dozen drinks later, they start staggering around the dance floor like total zombies. Familiar with this outcome? One wedding took it a few thrilling steps further… When Michael Jackson's 'Thriller' started to play, the best man hit the dancefloor and started to shuffle in classic drunk-guest mode. Soon he was being joined by the bridesmaids, then even the bride and groom themselves as the opening bars of the classic Jackson song played out. Then to the shock and amazement of the guests not in the know, the entire bridal party suddenly snapped into synchronised dance steps instantly recognisable from the 'Thriller' video… It turned out they had been practising for weeks; luckily it was captured for posterity and quickly posted on YouTube.

"Should there be dancing at a wedding, it is proper for the bride to open the first quadrille with the best man, the groom dancing with the first bridesmaid. It is not, however, very customary for a bride to dance, or for dancing to occur at an evening wedding." M.E.W. Sherwood, *Manners & Social Usage*, 1884

Several countries have the 'money dance' as an integral part of their ceremony… whereby, as the couple have their first dance, the guests pin money to them: a tradition that ranges as far

as Cyprus, Spain, Poland and Hawaii.

We're fools whether we dance or not, so we might as well dance. – Japanese Proverb

Save The First Dance For Me: Today's Top Ten 'First Dance' Wedding Songs

Don't Wanna Miss a Thing – Aerosmith
Everything I Do (I Do it for You) – Bryan Adams
Amazed – Lonestar
You're Still The One – Shania Twain
From This Moment – Shania Twain
Have I Told You Lately – Van Morrison
You're Beautiful – James Blunt
Truly, Madly, Deeply – Savage Garden
Angels – Robbie Williams
I Will Always Love You – Whitney Houston

"Dancing is the perpendicular expression of a horizontal desire." – George Bernard Shaw (1856-1950)

"Marriage is not a ritual or an end. It is a long, intricate, intimate dance together and
nothing matters more than your own sense of balance and your choice of partner."

Amy Bloom, writer

*"No matter what kind of music you ask them to play, your
wedding band will play it in such a way that it sounds like,
'New York, New York'"*

Dave Martin

Famously Unconsummated Marriages:

- Prince Arthur (Henry VIII's older brother) & Catherine of Aragon
- King Henry VIII & Ann of Cleves: having only seen her (over-flattering) picture before marriage, Big Hal decided she was too ugly for him to go through with it
- Catherine & Peter the Great
- John Ruskin & Euphemia Gray (so horrified was he to discover that women had pubic hair)
- Two of Rudolf Valentino's marriages
- Two of Zsa Zsa Gabor's marriages
- Louis XVI & Marie Antoinette – well, it took them seven years to get their act together

Ireland's oldest and most adventurous newlyweds – 85 and 93 years old on their wedding day – set off on their honeymoon, armed with vitamin pills, denture tablets and sensible slip-on shoes. Otherwise they packed light because their honeymoon was in…a camper van, travelling over 1,600 miles. "Well, we didn't want to go on a cruise," said the octogenarian bride, an unlikely candidate for being a hippy, "that's what old people do."

"In Hollywood, marriage is a success if it outlasts milk." – Rita Rudner

Three weeks after her wedding day, a bride calls her vicar. "Reverend!" she wails, "We've had the most DREADFUL fight!" "Calm down, my child," says the vicar. "It's not that bad. Every marriage has to have its first fight." "I know, I know!" gasps the bride. "But what am I going to do with the BODY?"

Blink And You Miss 'em: Short-Lived Celebrity Marriages:

- **Six hours:** Rudolph Valentino & Jean Acker
- **One day:** Zsa Zsa Gabor & Hub No.8, Adolf Hitler & Eva Braun, Britney Spears & Jason Alexander
- **One week:** Dennis Hopper & Michelle Phillips
- **Nine days:** Cher & Greg Allman
- **One month:** Burt Lancaster & June Ernst
- **Four months:** Renee Zellweger & Kenny Chesney

Can't Take You Anywhere: What The Wedding Guest Gets Up To:

• Even the wedding planner has to let her hair down occasionally – like the one caught kissing a guest on the dance floor by the groom's mother, who then congratulated her on 'getting into the spirit of the party'…

• One guest managed to pull not once but twice at the same wedding – each time at the back of the shrubbery that was the father-of-the-bride's pride and joy. He compounded his cheek by boasting about both escapades to the bride – then proceeded to discuss in front of her, entirely straight-faced, the benefits of "bedding-down" (roses) with the shrubbery-owning father…

• One guest owned up to having it away with the magician that had been booked to entertain the guests at the reception. History does not relate what sort of rabbit he pulled out of his hat for her…

• Two married guests had obviously missed the bit about the sanctity of marriage during the wedding ceremony… as they propositioned the wedding photographer to 'swing' with them and, even when she turned them down, carried on giving her the wink all night…

• This story was told to us as 'the one where the bride got into bed with me naked'… the bride had offered two old friends, both boys, her own room after the reception, since she was booked into a hotel and obviously wasn't going to be using it. By the end of the night, they were top-and-tailing in her childhood double bed, when they heard her coming into the room without turning the light on. The two boys weren't initially sure whether she had just come in looking for her stuff so stayed quiet, but she stripped and lurched over to the bed. 'Mark sweetie?' she slurred, slipping under the covers, obviously looking for her new husband. 'No, it's Pete,' squeaked Pete. 'And Fred,' said a small voice from the other end.

Knowing How To Make An Exit:

"A favorite dress for traveling is heliotrope cashmere, with bonnet to match. For a dark bride, nothing is more becoming than dark blue, made with a white vest and a sailor collar."
You tell'em, *Harper's Bazaar*, 1885

It is said that the old boots and cans tied to a couple's going-away car also hark back to the missiles thrown at the bride's family by the groomsmen when, in the event of a bride-capture, they tried to obstruct the newlyweds' getaway.

"Never go to bed mad. Stay up and fight."
Phyllis Diller

"Marry rich. Buy him a pacemaker. Then stand behind him and say, 'Boo!'"
Joan Rivers

"An occasional lucky guess as to what makes a wife tick is the best a man can hope for.
Even then, no sooner has he learned how to cope with the tick than she tocks."
Ogden Nash (1902-1971)

Our Best 'Going-Away' Stories:

• A high society wedding in Oxfordshire should have culminated in our happy couple leaving in a pony and trap. But a hunting horn, sounded to give the signal that the newlyweds were leaving, startled the pony into rearing up and throwing the designer-clad couple into a muddy ditch.

• As our newlyweds tucked themselves into their chauffeur-driven car, the mother of the bride leant through the back window to give some last-minute kisses or advice. Not knowing she was still there, the chauffeur moved off, automatically closing the back windows – failing to realise that her scarf had become trapped and that she was having to scurry along beside the car…

• The reception was on the banks of the Thames and the bride and groom sailed away in a tiny boat, into the darkness of the open river. Little did they know that the best man had secretly set up an awesome fireworks display on the opposite bank. As the sky erupted into brightness, the couple could suddenly be seen again – now down in the gunwales of the boat, getting down to some serious horizontal necking…

• In the days when everyone wore hats at a wedding, the crowd gathered round to watch the couple go away – in a helicopter. As the rotors gathered pace, the frantic scramble to hold onto one's hat left skirts and dresses unattended. "We suddenly realised that maybe we had told everyone to stand a little bit close," said a jubilant usher afterwards. "Everywhere the eye could see, skirts were being whipped overhead: it was a pants fest!"

• Setting off paper lanterns, glowing with the light of the candle inside, has become a popular finale to today's fashionable wedding. One such send-off, however, really brought the house down, when two of the lanterns landed on thatched-roof houses in a German suburb and caused £250,000 of fire damage: not quite the fiery end to the evening that the couple had hoped for.

• The bunfight for the bride's bouquet is infamous, but one couple's attempt to buck the trend ended in disaster. The ambitious plan was for a friend of the family to go up in a micro-light, fly over the wedding guests and launch the bride's bouquet from mid-air into the outstretched arms of the spinsters below (or just knock them out with it). Instead the bouquet was swept into the tail rotor, the motor blew up and the aircraft crashed. Luckily no-one died but afterwards guests were heard to say that only a real tosser could have come up with that idea…

• One of our couples left in an open-topped classic car for their hotel nearby. Nearly there, they got pulled over by the police. The groom was breathalysed and slammed in jail overnight.

"He married the woman to stop her getting away. Now she's there all day."
Philip Larkin, 'Self's The Man', Whitsun Weddings, 1964

*"Being married to Marge is like being married to my best friend
— with feeling boobs thrown in for free."*
Homer Simpson

*"Saying goodbye doesn't mean anything. It's the time we spent together
that matters, not how we left it."*

Tweek speaking to Craig, South Park, 1999

And They Lived Happily Ever After:

"Why do they not allow the bride to cross the threshold of the home herself, but lift her over? Is it because brides were originally carried off by force, or is it to make it appear that it is only under constraint that she enters the house where she is [presumably] to lose her virginity?" – Plutarch, *Moralia*: The Roman Questions, AD 95

Don't talk to one of our couples about the luck involved in carrying the bride across the threshold. The groom tripped as he hoisted his lady love over the doorstep, bashing his eye on the door knob as he fell, and elbowing his bride in her face. On the plane to their honeymoon destination, they sported matching black eyes…

"Life has taught us that love does not consist in gazing at each other but in looking outward together in the same direction." – Antoine de Saint-Exupery (1900-1944)

Have you ever looked back upon your wedding day, wishing you could do it all again? One couple went a step further – when their wedding photographs were lost in the post, they decided to recreate the entire day, purely for the cameras. Even more unbelievably, because the parcel of photos was insured, the insurers agreed to foot the entire £9,000 bill…

"I'm starting to realize why everyone says your wedding day is the best day of your life. It's not the coming together of friends and family. It's because finally, finally, the organizing is over, you can tear up your lists, set light to the copies of You & Your Wedding and luxuriate in the knowledge that you will never have to have a complete stranger squish your chest into a corset ever again…" – columnist Annabel Thorpe

"Love has nothing to do with what we are expecting to get – only what you are expecting to give, which is everything." Katharine Hepburn (1907-2003)

Marge: "Homer, is this the way you pictured married life?" Homer: "Yeah, pretty much, except we drove around in a van solving mysteries." – The Simpsons

"My most brilliant achievement was to persuade my wife to marry me."
Winston Churchill (1874-1965)

We'd Like To Raise A Glass To:

All our brides

and
Anthony Weldon
Eddie Ephraums
Tara Palmer-Tomkinson
Fi Kirkpatrick
Fiona Clare
Lizzie Patterson
Mark Cook
Covergirl Mel Culross (for getting them out)
Michelle at Silhouettes Bridal and Evening Wear, Richmond
Adrian Harvey

And, of course… The Dame